Real Miracles

For Normal People

■ ■ ■

By Prince Handley

University of Excellence Press

Copyright © 2016 by Prince Handley
All Rights Reserved.

UNIVERSITY OF EXCELLENCE PRESS
Los Angeles ▪ London ▪ Tel Aviv

ISBN-13: 978-0692642528

ISBN-10: 0692642528

First Edition

✠

The only Real Miracles book you need!

INTRODUCTION

This book will tell you about REAL MIRACLES that have happened in **different sectors of society**. These are **true accounts of REAL MIRACLES** that were unique—God appointed—interventions into both private and public affairs. You will learn about **thoughts from God and how to use them.** We will also discuss:

- Ideas and miracles
- Ideas and associates
- Miracles in office work
- Miracles in construction
- Miracles in public schools
- Miracles in the Sinai Desert
- Miracles in the Postal Service
- Miracles at the Jerusalem Hilton
- Miracles during travel for ministry
- Miracles while crash landing at LAX
- Children and miracles: why God works

In all of these I was blessed to be **a participant**. But the greatest part is **how God used them** to reach people with His MIRACLE power, and in many cases to **reach**

multitudes with the Good News of Messiah Jesus! **None of these happened in church or synagogue**.

Along the way you will discover the intent of God—actually, the heart of God—in doing MIRACLES for you—for normal people—and for His glory.

There is a KEY—a secret—you may observe as you journey through this book concerning MIRACLES. See if you can discover it.

FOREWORD

Would you like to learn about **HOW God visits normal, everyday people with His POWER?**

I'm talking about experiencing His MIRACLES—real miracles—in the **activities of business, education, construction, travel and engineering**.

This book is **NOT about divine encounters that have happened in synagogue or church**—or, so-called "religious" meetings.

It is also NOT about being healed when you're ready to die, or blind eyes opening or walking out of wheel chairs. These miracles of healing are covered in several of my other books. This book is about God dealing in commerce, education, work and play. It is about **real miracles** that happen to normal people in normal life.

You will learn HOW to expect God to enter your environment with MIRACLES—and, sometimes with the help of Holy Angels. Happenings that could NOT produce the results you need without some "outside" force sent by God.

In this book you will learn about the REAL FORCE—**the God force**—that will show up **to produce the miraculous ... and bring healing and deliverance** to not only individuals, but whole sectors of society.

There is a **SECRET KEY** contained in this book that will allow you to **unlock the door** to REAL MIRACLES. Read closely … and it will be revealed to YOU.

Let the FORCE be with YOU …

Real Miracles

For Normal People

■ ■ ■

IDEAS FROM GOD

Let's start this book with discussion about **IDEAS from God and how to be a good steward of them**. Some of the ideas that God gives you may be very foolish to others. At first they may even seem foolish to you, but you must be a good steward of whatever God gives you. **If God gives you an idea, then develop that idea.**

Also, **sometimes ideas are not for you**. They're for other people. God gives them to you to share with others, so—remember—you must be a good steward of the ideas that God gives you.

I remember I had an idea one time about making outdoor posters—weatherproof posters—for the Lord and I wanted to run the idea by somebody. I chose a person to run the idea by who I thought was the farthest out person in the world: a Canadian named Jacob. I ran the idea by him and he told me, *"This idea is too far out for me."* When Jacob told me that, **I knew the idea was from God.**

You see, my friend, God wants to do some things through your life that are so far out that nobody can receive the credit except God. You can't get the credit. **God gets the credit for the idea.**

When the idea came to me about the weatherproof outdoor posters I had envisioned them in different languages, so I planned to do them in bilingual Hebrew/English. I also did them in French, in Portuguese, in Spanish, in German and also in English. I selected 3 different basic sizes. One was a very small size, a 3 inch by 4 inch. The other one was 6 inch by 10 inch and the large one was about 30 inches by 40 inches.

As with any idea, you must first implement. I rented facilities across the street from where I lived and we did our own silk screening. After we would silk screen these in multi-colors, we would also put a chemical coating over them to protect them from the weather. The material—the base stock upon which we did the silk screening—was both a **weatherproof and tear-proof material**.

The signs became quite popular and the idea was successful. We received pictures of them from other countries—they went into many countries. They had different messages on them. One would have **"Appearing Here Soon,"** with the background of the world or the globe and then **"Messiah Jesus."** We had lots of different messages on them. The one in Hebrew was a star of David and it was in bilingual Hebrew-English, where it said, **"Messiah died for us ... was buried ... is alive."** On my next trip to Israel, I took in about 4,000 of these signs.

While I was in the airport in Boston waiting to go to Israel, I was paged on the loudspeaker to come to the customs office. A customs officer met me in the customs office and he said, *"What are these?"* They had all 4000 of the Hebrew-English signs there but he was only inquiring about the small 3 x 4 inch mini-signs. God spoke to me and said, *"Do not lie to this man."* I knew I had to be honest and I was searching for whatever I could say to be honest and I said, *"They're advertising samples."* He said, *"That's okay,"* in so many words and gave the approval for them.

When I got into Israel at Lod Airport, I stayed all night that first night in Tel Aviv and then I rented a car and drove down to Jerusalem where I booked a room to stay for a few days. Then I rented a car for approximately 7 weeks. I took these signs all over Israel. I put one sign up in the caves where the Dead Sea Scrolls had been found.

I spoke in Israel to several groups in the old city where I met, at the same time, several Israeli Arabs. They were Arab Christians who loved the Lord, who loved Israel, and who loved the Jews. One of them was named named Ramsey Hassim. He was a Palestinian Arab, but he was a Christian. He was a believer in Jesus, the Mashiach. He loved these signs that I had, especially the small 3 by 4 inch ones.

I gave hundreds of these signs to Mr. Hassim and he gave some to another Arab Christian. The other Arab Christian—I don't know why—was wearing an army fatigue jacket. In the Israeli army at that time, if you were well known—that is, if they knew your family background—you could be in the military. But this young man was not in the military. He simply had a fatigue jacket on. They arrested him. When they arrested him, they found all these signs in the pockets of his fatigue jacket that said **"Messiah died for us ... was buried ... is alive" with the star of David on them**. The soldiers detained him and took took him to the police station where the police asked him what the signs were about.

He started preaching to them about Yeshua—the Messiah of Israel—and they liked it. They liked the signs, so the policemen put the signs up on the wall of the police station. **These were permanent signs!** There was no way to get them down unless you chiseled OR unless you blew up the wall. The Israeli soldiers in the **IDF**—the Israeli Defense Force—liked the signs, also, and they then affixed the signs to the stocks of their weapons—on their rifles. **These were permanent signs!**

These signs were all over Israeli. I shared this story with you to show what can be accomplished with an IDEA that God gives you. **Do it or share it. Be a good steward.** Also in another subsequent session, **I'll share with you how God reach multiplied millions of people through these signs**.

Be a good steward of what God gives you. Keep your mind open. **God wants to reach people with His love more than you do.** We're living in the last days so listen to the ideas that the Holy Spirit gives you and then implement them—or at least share them with others—so that they may implement them. God will do miraculous works through you.

IDEAS AND MIRACLES

In this chapter we will discuss **Ideas and Miracles**. In the previous chapter we talked to you about the poster idea God gave me where we had Gospel signs: small signs 3 by 4 inches, medium sized 10 by 12 inches, and large size 30 by 40 inch. These were all weatherproof, outdoor signs and when we put them up, **they were permanent—and I mean permanent**. If you wanted to take one off a building, you had to either scrape them off or tear the wall down from the building. These signs reached multiplied millions of people for Messiah.

I told you in the last chapter how I took in—I didn't say "smuggled"—I took in about 4,000 of the smaller signs, plus the larger sizes. I mentioned how God got me through customs and how several of the smaller signs ended up in the police station in Jerusalem. Soldiers in the **IDF**—Israeli Defense Forces—also placed them on the stocks of their weapons and the police put them up on the walls of the police station. And remember … **they were permanent.**

I want to tell you some other things that happened with these signs. On the very large signs—the 30 x 40 inch ones—we had a special glue we would use. Not only were they waterproof but they also had a protective coating over them to keep them from fading, so they could stay up for years. And … **they were permanent.**

I had an associate that worked with me in the silk screening process and we had different ideas that we shared with each other. During this time, in downtown

Los Angeles—somewhere between 3rd and 6th Streets and around Figueroa Street—they were doing lots of excavation and huge construction. At that time they were building the Twin Towers—the ARCO Towers—also, the Bonaventure Hotel. **This was a giant project**.

At the construction site—a whole city block square—they had large promo signs which would list the architects, engineers, and contractors. **These promo credits were strategically placed by the Lord**. One of the promo signs was on the southeast and one on the southwest side of this giant hole in the ground project. They were placed perfectly as a backdrop upon which to place our large 30 x 40 inch posters.

One night, my associate and I drove to downtown Los Angeles about 3 AM. We pulled up in a van and took ladders out of the van. We worked on both the easterly portion and the westerly portion, and we had to work fast to avoid being noticed. We unrolled these signs. Like I said—these were the large 30 x 40 inch signs. We had to apply the glue—**the special miracle glue that would never let them come off**. I remember we got the easterly portion done. Beautiful sign. It was the sign that said, **"Appearing here soon: Jesus Christ."** On the other, westerly, side of this big project we put up the sign with the **Star of David** that said**, "Messiah died for us … Was buried … Is alive."**

When we were working on the westerly portion—all of a sudden a police paddy wagon drives up. **We had already prayed that God would blind the police if they saw us**. Well … the police paddy wagon was about

10 feet from us and waiting for a red light to change. The light seemed like it lasted for eternity. We're right there within "spitting" distance of the police van. I remember I'm holding onto the sign up on the ladder and I think my associate was using the squeegee to smooth it out with the glue between it and the structure. (I'm reminding God that we asked him to blind the police—not to hurt them but that they wouldn't see us.)

We were so close to the police wagon that the policeman could have heard me if I sneezed. He was about 10 feet from me with an open door on the side of the paddy wagon. He never turned his head one second. He seemed like a mannequin. I stood there on the ladder while I'm holding that sign up in front of him—right beside him—and then the traffic light changed and the policeman drove off.

The Lord was with us. Those signs stayed up there well over a year while the construction commenced until they had to take the promo structures down for landscaping and other reasons. **Multiplied millions of people were reached through these signs**. Not only cars and public transit vehicles but, also, pedestrian traffic. We probably had millions of dollars of free advertising there, and these structures were—must have been—designed by God before we used them. The promo structures were perfect for showing our signs and reaching people for the LORD.

When you have an idea from God, the Holy Spirit will go ahead of you—and prepare things for you so that what you do will be coordinated and timed perfectly. The logistics will flow together AND the good news of Messiah will flow to the public and to the nations. **In this case, Israel, also!**

In a subsequent chapter, I'm going to tell you how I put up a big billboard in downtown Los Angeles right on the route where some of the wealthiest Jews in the world have to travel everyday. It was a tremendous miracle—and I give all the credit to the LORD.

I hope what I have shared with you encourages you to listen to God and receive his ideas. And, to implement the ideas—or at least share them with others. If the idea is not for you, God wants you to be a good steward and share it with somebody else. Remember ... **the anointing of the Holy Spirit is resident in or upon an idea**—with the result that **the yoke of the enemy is broken as the IDEA from the LORD is released**. The Good News is for the world.

God has many IDEAS to give YOU—and many MIRACLES to do through those ideas—as you either share them or implement them.

IDEAS AND ASSOCIATES

In the Tanakh, the Jewish Scriptures, the Bible tells us in Proverbs 13:20, *"He that walks with wise men shall be wise. But a companion of fools shall be destroyed."* If you want to improve your judgment and the ability to make quick decisions, choose out wise associates. I pray for myself and my children everyday that God will give us his choice of associates.

Sometimes prayers take a while. **You should want only God's choice of associates**. That doesn't mean you don't love other people. That doesn't mean you don't interact with other people. But your close associates— those that are your key associates—you want them to be God's choice for you.

Years ago, when I started a nonprofit corporation, I prayed that God would lead me in the selection of directors. I have had several people on my Board of Directors through the years. God has directed me to wonderful godly people. I remember three in particular. One was name Ed Lindquist. He had been associated with Grey Advertising in Detroit, and they did all of Ford's advertising. Another one was Al Hagen, who was Director of Marketing for Toyota in the Untied States. Another one was Magdy Girgis—Mike Girgis—my Egyptian friend, whose father was one of the third wealthiest men in Egypt. His father had more political power than Abdul Nasser had when he was President of Egypt.

My friend Magdy had to be smuggled out of Egypt because he became a Christian, and they had him on the black list for "trying to Christianize the nation." He paid some Druze to smuggle him out of the country and through Syria where he finally was able to get to the USA. When Magdy Girgis came to the United States he could not obtain a job because he had never worked. He was educated—he was an engineer—but he had no work experience. He was wealthy. They had a stable of about 15 automobiles at their home in Egypt. Finally he obtained some employment by cleaning out restrooms. Ultimately, he finally found work as an engineer at Hughes Aircraft.

These men were key to me. They were associates. We didn't spend a lot of time together, but the time we spent was very critical and crucial. As a matter of fact, Ed Lindquist went on to start his own nonprofit corporation. He gave me a large sum of money to be used for the ministry; however, I gave it back to him. I told him, *"Ed, for some reason God wants me to give you this money back to you."* My friend, it's important to obey the Holy Spirit. Money isn't everything. **The whole world is not about money. The whole world is about God.** *"You cannot serve God and money,"* the Scriptures tell us. You put God first. There is nothing evil about money, like there is nothing evil with the television. It's what you do with it. The Bible never says money is evil. It says, *"The love of money is the root of all evil."*

I listened to God and gave the money back—quite a sum of money—to Ed Lindquist. He used it to start his own nonprofit corporation. We need to be sensitive to the leading of the Holy Spirit. We need to discern what is of God, and what is NOT of God. We also need to discern what God wants us to receive and what God does NOT want us to receive. **Everyday I pray that God will give me discernment over people, things, and situations**. We are in the world, but not of it, and we must have discernment.

I originally started the nonprofit corporation for the LORD **with the purpose of starting churches and spreading God's Word via the media**. I had a vision while I was preaching in the open air one time. It was not an ocular vision, but a mental vision. While I was preaching in the open air I had a great anointing on me. I probably had been fasting, I don't remember. But while I was preaching, my heart was crying out to God. I was reaching multitudes—reaching thousands—that day ministering in the open air. My heart was crying out *"Lord, how can I reach the whole world."* God spoke to me while I was speaking to these crowds. God answered me, *"Through the media."* Then, the LORD began to give me different ideas.

One time, the LORD gave me an idea of **"Billboards for Jesus."** This idea encompassed designing different sizes and models of outdoor billboards … and supplying people with blueprints and building instructions for putting up their own billboards. The Lord gave me this idea, but I didn't really know how to implement it. I called together a body of men. I met with Magdy "Mike" Girgis and several other men like Ed Linquist. Also, several engineers who worked together at Hughes Aircraft. One of the men at Hughes in the Engineering Department was also a cartoonist. **I shared my idea with these men**. We were there maybe just an hour in that meeting. They each had a different assignment to do. We met again, in about two weeks. It was fantastic what these men put together. **I had—as I remember—seven different billboard plans**.

These were all engineers, and I worked with another engineer, a Civil Engineer, who was head of the City of Placentia Planning Department. He approved these plans, and put his stamp of approval and certified the plans. They were all safe and sound. We had a mini plan, and we had a maxi plan, and we had plans in between. People could choose which plans they wanted to build. **They were successful because the cartoonist put together a brochure describing the plans, and how people could reach the multitudes of their community with the billboards**.

It was a tremendous brochure, a beautiful brochure. Each model, plan, and sizes were dynamically illustrated, and the cartoonist did a lot of good artwork in between the pages. I remember a retired U.S. Air Force officer received one of these brochures. He lived in the State of Maine in the USA. He built and paid for five (5) **Billboards for Jesus** on highways right in his area. These were a great success.

One of my associates—and for whom I held a Bible study in his home—had a high level position in Pacific Telephone prior to the AT&T breakup in 1984. He went with me to the Planning Commission Department in Los Angeles. I had previously received a communication with a Spanish pastor in downtown Los Angeles who pastored a church right where the Harbor Freeway and the Santa Monica Freeway merge, **right in the key hub of the downtown LA metroplex**. He wanted to put up a **Billboard for Jesus**.

I went down to Los Angeles and met with him. We had a special plan drawn up for the billboard he wanted to erect. This required a special light that was 24 feet (8 meters) long so the billboard could be lighted and seen at night. I found only one place that had a light just like we needed for this particular design. It was somewhere in the state of Utah in the western part of the Untied States. I ordered the light. **It was very expensive and I did not have the money**. Nobody knew that I owed this money. When the day came for the money to be paid on the light, miraculously **the money came in to the dollar** (and I think maybe the penny) to pay for the sign.

The light was shipped to Los Angeles. The billboard was erected on top of the Spanish church. The sign was finished—ready to go—with the light on top of this big giant billboard in downtown Los Angeles. **BUT ... I had to get the plan approved by the city**. My associate, Wally, from Pacific Bell went up with me up to the Planning Department in Los Angeles. I think we were on either the third floor or fifth floor (I don't remember). The inspector looked at the plans, and said, *"You can't do this. This goes against codes and laws five different*

20

ways." Remember … we already had a lot of time and expense in the project. We had started in faith.

First of all, on a billboard site in that busy area of L.A., you could only have ID on the billboard, in other words, the identification of the sign. You just couldn't put up any message. The message on this sign was very plain. A **Star of David** and it said *"Messiah Jesus is God, our salvation."* Also, it violated city codes because there was an ordinance stating that signs could not be nearer than so may feet to the freeway and **ours was just hugging right up against it but overhead**. Also, because of the lighting AND the size, there was also a zoning restriction against it. Plus, there was an ordinance requiring that only a maximum number of signs could be erected in a particular zone area. **Anyway, our sign violated five giant violations of Los Angeles city codes.** And, we had already built it and placed it.

Learn a lesson from this, my friend. **Never take "No!" for an answer**. The planning inspector said, *"You can't do this."* The sign violated CCR's—"Covenants, Codes and Restrictions"—five different ways. **I didn't say anything, I just looked at him.** I didn't say one word. I don't know how much time went by. Finally, the man said, *"Let me go upstairs and check with someone."* I don't know how much time went by but it was at least 20 minutes. The man finally came back to the desk and he said, *"It's all approved."*

My associate from Pacific Telephone, Wally, about had a heart attack. He couldn't believe it. He told me later, *"I have never seen—not only such a miracle—but such a series of miracles in so short a time."* This was an impossibility five different ways. **God is the God of the impossible**. In Jeremiah 32:27, we read, *"Behold I am the LORD God of all flesh. Nothing is too hard for me."*

My friend, **never take "No!" for an answer**. **The billboard reached multiplied millions of people—tens of thousands everyday—through the years: day and night**. What I didn't tell you is this: At the particular place where this billboard was—in key traffic time, not only morning and evening, and even throughout the middle part of the day—traffic would just creep around, "stop and go" slowly around this sign because there was usually a bottle neck in traffic flow there. They would see this sign with the **Star of David** that said, *"Messiah Jesus is God our salvation."*

By the way, this billboard was located in a particular area **where some of the wealthiest Jews in the world had to drive by everyday**. This is the main thoroughfare through downtown Los Angeles as it turned off going out to Westwood, Beverly Hills, Rodeo Drive, Brentwood, and other areas. The God of Abraham, Isaac and Jacob knew this ahead of time and I just "happened" to be blessed with the IDEA.

When God gives you an idea, you need to make sure that you're a good steward of the IDEA. When God gives you a good idea, realize that there will be MIRACLES attached to it—there will be an anointing upon **and resident in** that idea by the Holy Spirit.

When God gives you an idea—if it is for YOU—if you don't know how to do it, then you need to choose wise companions—wise associates—to help you implement the idea. We need to have a Spirit of Excellence in everything that we attempt to accomplish for the Lord.

MIRACLES IN INDUSTRY

I want to talk to you in this section about **Miracles in Industry**. I mentioned in the previous section, **Ideas and Associates**, that one of the members on my board of directors was a man named Magdy Girgis or Mike Girgis, who was from Egypt. His father had been the third wealthiest man in Egypt. His father actually had more power politically than Nasser did when Nasser was in office.

My friend Mike was on the blacklist in Egypt allegedly for trying to Christianize the nation. He had to be smuggled out of the country and across the hills in Syria by the Druze and then finally got out of Syria to the United States. My Egyptian friend was one of the greatest Christians I have ever known: he loved Jesus.

Mike worked in the Engineering Department at Hughes Aircraft in Fullerton, California. Several of the men that I knew who worked there had Bible studies every morning. There was a real awakening in Hughes Aircraft at the Fullerton division as well as the Hughes plant near the Los Angeles LAX airport. These brothers would meet early before they went to work at 8:00 in the morning and hold bible studies in the engineering office. They had bible studies in the morning and also at Noon.

One of the brothers at the Hughes Fullerton Division was a prophet. His name was Jack Angel (that was his real name). He was a real man of God—a real prophet of God—and his little daughter was born with clubbed feet. When the girl was around 7 years of age, Jack took his daughter to a shoe store and he told the salesman there he wanted to buy a pair of shoes for the girl. The shoe salesman looked at the girl's clubbed feet and saw they were turned in. He said, *"We don't sell corrective shoes here."* Jack said to the salesman, *"That's okay, Jesus is going to heal her."*

He told him what size he wanted and the salesman picked out the shoes and got ready to package them up. But the girl's father said**, "No, I want to put them on her now. Jesus is going to heal her now."** The manager of the store was really flabbergasted. He couldn't believe that God still did miracles today. Jack took the shoes, set the little girl down and prayed over her in Jesus' name ... and all of a sudden one on the feet straightened out. Then the other foot went right into position—became normal—and the girl's father put the shoes on her. **The little girl walked out of the shoe store with perfectly healed feet, new shoes and a happy heart**.

That's the kind of miracles that happened regularly at Hughes Aircraft. They invited me in to minister in the Engineering Department. Next, they invited me to come a second time. The next time I went to preach at Hughes Aircraft in Fullerton the Lord had already been working not only in the Engineering Department but also in the factory. There was standing room only where I was ministering. During one of the Noon prayer meetings a fellow named Walter Meisenbach came up to my friends and he said, *"What is this born-again stuff you guys keep talking about?"*

Walter had been a hunchback for 15 years. He was in serious pain everyday—all the time—continually. The men at the Bible study shared the Good News of Messiah Jesus with Walter. He received Jesus as his Messiah—was born again right there in the Noon Bible study—and then they laid hands on Walter and asked the Lord Jesus to heal Walter ... to deliver Walter from being a hunchback from this bent over condition he had for 15 years.

All of a sudden, "Pop, pop, pop, pop, pop." **They could hear his spine popping. Walter straightened right up and had a perfectly normal spine**. When Walter arrived home that night, his wife was near the door when he came in. She looked at him and she saw the shine on his face. Not only was he joyous because he had met Jesus, but he was joyous because he was no longer carrying around that pain he had for 15 years. Plus, he was standing straight up. This had a tremendous effect on the whole family.

Well it was sometime later, during the next year, I was invited to preach in a public high school. There were so many drug problems in the public schools that I had been invited by several public schools to come minister to the students. They wanted help. They didn't even care if it was Jesus that helped them. No prayer or Bible studies—but please send Jesus—we need help.

While I was ministering in one large public high school, I felt impressed to share about Walter Meisenbach's MIRACLE healing. I did NOT know any of the students or faculty there. While I was telling them about the healing in Walter's spine, one of the girls spoke up and said, *"Oh, that's my daddy. Let me tell you the rest of the story."* She began to tell what happened at home when her father came home after being healed.

These were some of the kind of miracles that happened at Hughes Aircraft—where people would just get together and pray and read the Holy Bible. They were men and women, engineers, secretaries, factory workers ... all reading the Word of God, worshiping God and allowing the Holy Spirit to come into their midst. Then ... the Messiah Jesus would do the miraculous.

That is all that is required. Don't make it too hard. Miracles in industry, miracles in marketing, miracles in business, miracles in education—God does miracles anywhere my friend. He promised in Jeremiah 33:3, ***"Call unto me and I will answer you, and I will show you great and mighty things you do not know."***

God can even do miracles in churches and synagogues. Just let him have his way.

MIRACLES IN PUBLIC SCHOOLS

I want to talk to you in this chapter about **miracles in education**. There was a period of time where I was being invited by lots of public high schools in the USA to come speak to their students. This happened almost weekly for a while. The drug situation was so bad in the high schools that these schools were actually calling me and asking me to come talk to their students. The US Supreme Court outlawed the Holy Bible from being read in school and outlawed public prayer in the schools but **the public schools needed help—and they heard that Jesus could help them**.

At one high school, I was meeting with students in the science auditorium. I remember at all these high schools, at every one of them—even the ones where I spoke at in other countries—God would always give me a Word of Knowledge for certain students. A Word of Knowledge—one of the gifts of the Holy Spirit—is where God shows you a situation about a person or about a situation. The Word of Knowledge is one of the gifts of the Holy Spirit—sometimes it's a dual gift—where there's a combination of the Word of Knowledge, and the Word of Wisdom.

The Word of Knowledge is where the Holy Spirit reveals to you knowledge about a person or a situation. It's never to embarrass anyone, but it's to show people that God knows exactly what's going on with them—or what's involved in their life—so that He can help them. The Word of Wisdom operates in conjunction with the Word of Knowledge and the both gifts might operate through me or the second gift through another person—but the Word of Wisdom tells the person what to do—it provides wisdom in that situation—to alleviate a problem, or to bring deliverance, or to bring them in alignment to God's will. In other words, the **Word of Knowledge tells the person** (who is receiving the word) **about a situation in their life**. It is a "sign" to them that God knows what's going on … and the **Word of Wisdom tells them the answer: what to do about it to bring healing, success or deliverance.**

I remember in the science auditorium—it was a bowl-shaped auditorium—as I looked up to the right there was a girl about 17 and God gave me a Word of Knowledge for her. I called her down to the front where I was standing. She told me immediately, *"I don't believe in God or Jesus."* As I remember, she told me that she hated Jesus.

Anyway, I told her, *"Well, that's all right, Jesus loves you and I love you, and God's going to do a miracle for you today."* God gave me a Word of Knowledge about a situation in her life. I don't remember the specifics, but I think it was a medical condition or a physical condition. **God instantly touched her, healed her, gave her a miracle, and she received Jesus into her life**.

I received a phone call later that day and somebody told me that this girl had been the biggest bad mouth of the Lord on that campus. She used to go around just telling everybody how she hated the Lord, how the Lord was not good, and just mouthing off bad things about God. That day after God did the miracle for her—and after the

Holy Spirit gift of the Word of Knowledge operated in her life—**she was going all over that campus telling people about Jesus, and his love for her, and her love for Jesus**.

Now, here's something ironic. The same day I spoke at that high school I received a phone call from a pastor. He was a Presbyterian pastor and he told me, *"You know, there's a Christian group on that campus and they're mad that you've been there." "They've been working there for years to try to reach students for the Lord and you come in and all these stuff happens."* I thought, *"Stuff? You mean people coming to know the LORD, people hearing about the LORD, people receiving miracles and having their lives changed?"*

Anyway … it wasn't a week after that I received a call from another high school, and they wanted me to come talk to their students. Again, the drug situation was very bad in that high school. Right before I went to go preach at that high school—it was about an hour drive—I picked up the phone and called the Presbyterian pastor who had phoned me the previous week. I said, *"You know, I just received another request to come talk in another high school,"* and I said, *"I just want to check with you to see if it is okay to heal on The Sabbath."*

Now, it wasn't The Sabbath, but he got the idea. Remember—the biggest opposition to Jesus' life and miracles was from the religious crowd: the Pharisees, the Sadducees and the Scribes. Different times Jesus healed people right in front of them; and he asked the question, *"Is it okay to do good on The Sabbath? Who* among you doesn't unloose his cow and take him to drink water on The Sabbath?" The Presbyterian pastor got the idea and he never bothered me again.

In a previous section of this book I discussed the miracle experienced by Walter Meisenbach, the hunchback, who was healed instantly during lunch hour at Hughes Aircraft. When I told about that in another high school meeting, a young girl spoke up right away said, *"Oh, that's my daddy you're talking about."* She said, *"Let me tell you the rest of the story."* She said, *"When my daddy came home, my mum was right near the door when he came in. When my mother looked at my father, he was smiling, and was so happy that he had met Jesus and had no more pain after 15 years—he was standing up straight."* Then, the girl said, *"My mother and I—the whole family—have come to know The LORD."*

The Spirit of God fell on that group of students, and I started laying hands on people. I went over and laid hands on a bald-headed man—he was the Vice-Principal—while praying in tongues in the Holy Spirit's language over him. God began to do miracles. Later on I found out—somebody phoned me and told me—**that this man had come as a skeptic, but now was a believer in Jesus the Messiah**.

Years ago, while I was in Rhodesia (before it was Zimbabwe) I was invited to speak at several public schools with grade brackets corresponding to high school in the USA. **In every one of the schools where I ministered the gifts of the Holy Spirit operated and God performed MIRACLES**. At the first school where I ministered I taught on "Jesus, the Healer." At the end of my teaching, I started to pray for students … but nothing happened. **I asked God, *"What is wrong?"***

The LORD spoke to me and said, "***I don't want you to pray for the students. I want you to teach them HOW to pray for each other.*** *Because when you leave, they will just say, 'It was a white man who came to pray for us.'"* I did what God told me. **I began having the students lay hands on each other and every one I know of who needed healing was healed.** In every school I went to after that, I did the same thing. God would give me a Word of Knowledge about a condition in a student that I did NOT know (a condition in their body). I would call them out, and then have another student or students lay hands on them in Jesus' name and **they would always be healed.** Many students received Messiah Jesus as a result of witnessing the MIRACLES.

The saddest school where I went to minister was referred to as a "colored" school. The students were "mixed" from African and Caucasian backgrounds, with some having parents from India. You could feel the heaviness in the spirit of the students. **They were persecuted by both blacks and by whites**. But, praise God, after the Lord Jesus visited them they did NOT have that problem. **The spirit of heaviness was broken and they experienced the JOY of the LORD!**

My friend, God does miracles in business, in engineering, in marketing and in education … in every sector of society. Believe it or not, God even does miracles in churches and synagogues. Let the Holy Spirit have his way. Believe what God says, believe the Holy Bible. The Bible says, *"You have not, because you ask not."* **Ask God for what you need—ask God to help you—ask God to do the miracles that you need in life.** That's pre-conditioned on the fact that you want to live for God. I didn't say you're perfect, I said you want to live for God. You want to know God: you're normal. **That's why Yeshua (Jesus) came to earth—because you and I are not perfect—he came to pay for our imperfections.**

He came to pay for our sins so that we can have His life in us and to give us a desire to live for Him. Today, if you want to have **right-standing** in Heaven—*that's what the word **righteousness** means*—with right-standing before God, realize that Yeshua—The Messiah of Israel—took your sins upon Him and He gave you His righteousness in exchange. **He took YOUR sins and in exchange He gave YOU his righteousness**.

> *"For God has made Him to be sin for us, who knew no sin; that we might be made the righteousness of God in Him."* (2 Corinthians 5:21)

If you want to receive that wonderful forgiveness today, pray and ask Jesus, The Messiah of Israel, to come into your life, and to give you his life ... and then thank him for taking your sins upon him. You are forgiven!

King David described the blessedness of the person whose sins are forgiven—whose transgressions are wiped out—and who is right before God. (Psalm 32:1-2) David was an adulterer, and a murderer, and yet he repented before God and knew the joy of forgiveness.

My friend, I don't care what you've done, God loves you today. If you receive Jesus into your life, God can give you a new start. He will wipe away all your sins—remove them as far as the East is from the West—never to be remembered anymore. **You will have a brand NEW life of MIRACLES: real miracles!**

MIRACLES IN THE POSTAL SERVICE

I want to share with you now about **miracles in the postal service**. Yes, that's right, miracles in public mail: both domestic and international. I want to encourage you today by teaching you how the Holy Angels will help you when you're involved in God's Holy Work. In the work of disseminating—propagating—the word of God. Jesus taught us, *"What things so ever you desire—**when you pray**—believe you receive them."* I'm going to tell you about some MIRACLES that have happened in the postal service.

One time I was shipping out to over 100 countries in one day. I didn't have the funds to send the shipment by Express Mail. This was an important shipment. It involved reaching lots of people—multitudes of people—in different countries with the Word of God. We prayed over every one of the items being mailed. By surface mail, this should have taken five to six weeks to go into some of the countries—some a lot longer if the destination was back in the far away villages, very remote villages—but **I needed a fast response back**.

I prayed to the Lord and I asked God to have the Holy Angels assist in this mailing so it would get it to the people speedily and the responses would come back to me speedily. **I needed angelic intervention and I received it**. I needed to get this project that God had put on my heart expedited. It was designed to reach people with the message of Jesus the Messiah: how he can save, heal and deliver people and baptize them in the Spirit of God.

I got answers—responses—back in about a week. Now check this out. If you know anything about the postal mail—if you've ever been involved in international mail—the following had to be a MIRACLE. **In about a week the mail had already been to several countries and the mail had come back to me**. Figure that. Even the time for the people to sit down, write a letter or respond, go to the post office—which in many cases would be many miles, and some of the people may not even have the money for postage at the time.

If you've ever been overseas you know how poverty-stricken it is in many third world countries; however, in about a week I had responses back already. And remember, that was before the day of computers, internet and email—and, before Global Priority Mail. **Now why was that? Because I was involved in doing God's work and in doing God's will**. My friend, if there's anything that I've learned through the years, it's this: **If your plans fit into God's plans, you will have God's faith and God's faith always works.**

Years ago we used to mail out business reply cards inviting people to study our Free Bible Studies. Now **these were good for free return postage only in the United States**. In other words, they'd tear a card off wherever they saw it—whether it was in a bus or a laundromat or something they received in the mail—and they'd write in their name and address, requesting FREE Bible studies in the New Testament. They'd send it back and they did not have to pay postage. The cards would be retuned to us and we would pay the postage. We'd pay the postage when we picked it up at the post office.

Now these were only good within the confines of the United States. However, **I remember getting one from a 14-year-old Arab girl in Bethlehem**. Her name was Niya Aliss. **The card she sent back came all the way from Bethlehem**—out of Israel—across the continent of Europe, into the United States, into California, into the city of Downey. **It should never have been honored by the Postal Service**. I picked it up for a few pennies. We sent her Bible studies. She graduated from the Bible Study course, and became a fantastic Christian.

Now who do you think did that? God is in control. Angels are still alive today. But … demons are still alive today, also. **That's why Messiah Jesus—who's still alive today—delivers from demons today, still heals today, still saves today. He still baptizes people in the Holy Spirit of God**. Every one of the Gospels—plus the Book of Acts—tells us that Yeshua (Jesus) is the Baptizer in the Holy Spirit. He's a Savior. He's a Healer. He's a Deliverer. He's the soon-coming King to rule over the Kingdom of God here on Earth: the Messianic Kingdom for which the Jewish people have looked for centuries.

I've had a lot of other miracles in the postal service mail. Now … check this out. **I've received mail with my name on it—but no address**. I'm looking at a letter right now that I got the other day that had nothing on it. **It did NOT have my name. It had no address. It had no city, no state, no country, no zip code, nothing**. That letter

37

I'm looking at, **came from the country of Ghana**. In that letter, I'm opening it now, it had a picture of a man **handing out our gospel literature at a funeral way back in a village**. His name is Emmanuel Apau. I've been in that country many times. Along with that photograph is a request for more literature. The postal service identified this letter evidently because at the bottom of the envelope it says *"Christ's healing power."*

Finally, there have been unique—personal—miracles I have experienced in the Postal Service offices: one I will share with you here. One time I was in the outer box lobby (where the Post Office boxes were accessed) in the large Downey, California USA Post Office. Suddenly a lady was smitten with blindness and did not know where she was. She ran into the heavy glass doorway leading to the main lobby where the clerks were and hit her head on the door. As I remember she fell to the ground ... but nobody would help her. I went to her and laid hands on her in the name of Jesus and instantly her sight and senses returned.

My friend, God will do anything for you if you'll do anything for Him. Jesus said, *"Follow me and I will make you fishers of men."* He will help you fish ... if you want to catch men.

MIRACLES IN THE SINAI DESERT

I want to talk to you in this section of the book about "**Miracles in the Sinai Desert**." We discussed previously about "**Ideas from God and How to Use Them**." I mentioned how I smuggled—or delivered—4,000 of our Vis-Tab Bible signs into Israel. I told you how the Israeli policemen were putting the small size (3 x 4 inches) up on the walls of the jails and how the soldiers in the **IDF** (**I**sraeli **D**efense **F**orces) were putting them on the stocks of their weapons. (These mini signs had **permanent** adhesive on them, also.)

I want to talk to you, also, about **what happened when I put up our signs in the Sinai Desert**. I had been down in the area of Eilat, a resort area, and travelling south of there down the highway towards the direction of Egypt. I felt impressed to get out of my car and take a walk. I walked for a short distance towards the West. It may sound unbelievable ... but I ended up walking with camels—19 camels—for a while. There was no camel driver and they weren't carrying a burden. I don't know what they were doing there, unless they belonged to some Bedouin somewhere nearby in the desert. Camels are very expensive and I'm sure they weren't running loose, running unaccounted for—some where, some how. I learned later that it is dangerous to mess around with camels.

Anyway, while I was going through the desert, I was directed by the Holy Spirit to a large, sheet metal—stainless steel—assemblage. It was in the ground and I dismantled it. Inside, there were meters.

Evidently, the Israeli government had put those meters there and placed them so that they could detect—when it did rain in the desert—water flow.

Anyway, after I dismantled the assemblage around the meters, I fastened to the inside of the stainless steel structure my permanent adhesive Mini-Signs that were bilingual Hebrew and English. The signs had the **Star of David** on them and said, ***"Messiah, Yeshua, died for us. Was buried. Is alive."*** I assembled the parts back together, closed it off, and went on my way. I walked back to the highway and to my rental car. I decided instead of going to Egypt, that I would turn around and go northward. I just felt direction from the LORD to do it. After driving north—I don't know, maybe an hour or forty-five minutes—I saw an orange juice shack on the left. There weren't any businesses along the road, at least at that time, that year. There was a place where they sold orange juice, just in the middle of nowhere.

I pulled off and there was a tour bus there and a lot of young people. They were from a kibbutz. I stopped for orange juice and I was talking to a young Jewish man about Messiah Yeshua. I had a Jewish New Testament, the Brit Chadashah, with me. It was written in Hebrew or a prophetic version of the Hebrew scriptures. I talked to him about the Messiah and he asked me for the New Testament I had, so I gave it to him.

There had been a young man, probably in his early twenties, listening to my conversation while I had talked to the Jewish man. When I handed the young Jewish man the Hebrew New Testament, the fellow next to us

40

then said, *"I know you!—Dallas, Texas."* He mentioned my name. Then, he told me he had heard me speak at CFNI: Christ for the Nations Institute in Dallas, Texas.

After leaving the orange juice stand, I left and while driving on north I started thinking, *"What a foolish thing to do. To spend all that time taking apart that meter assemblage, putting up signs there. **It's probably NOT going to rain heavily in the desert for a long time, anyway ... at least, NOT flood."** [NOTE: It only rains **heavily** in the Negev about 3 or 4 days a year.] I thought, *"I don't know if I really listened to the Holy Spirit about that."*

About a year later I was speaking in Texas again at Christ for the Nations Institute. They love the Jews there and they've done a lot of work through the years to help Israel and Israeli people. While I was speaking, I felt impressed by the Spirit of God to tell about the time—along the highway in the Negev south of Eilat in the Sinai Peninsula—when I installed those signs.

After I was finished speaking, as I was leaving backstage, a young man ran up to me and he said, *"I was one of the people on the bus with the people from the kibbutz. I watched you as you talked to that Jewish fellow and I saw you give him the Jewish New Testament—and I said, 'I know you.'"* He said, *"That was me."* He said, **"Let me tell you the rest of the story. After you left, within a half an hour, a large flood came and we couldn't even travel. We had to wait for the flood waters to come down in the low parts of the highway."**

The God of Abraham, Isaac and Jacob wanted so much that somebody would come to those meters where I had placed a sign that **He made it flood the Sinai. I found later that it hadn't flooded the Sinai like that in two and a half years.** You see, my friend, the God of Israel promises that His word will never return to Him void. It will always accomplish the purpose for which He sent it.

Let me encourage you today. Distribute the Word of God in any process, media or form. Tell people what God says, because it is His Word that brings life and light. But ... let me share with you a POWER SECRET below.

REACH OUT TO THE JEWS AND ISRAEL

GOD WILL WORK WITH YOU IN MIRACLES

MIRACLES IN CONSTRUCTION

In this chapter I will talk to you about miracles that I have experienced pertaining to construction projects. Several years ago, the Lord gave me an idea to design plans for outdoor billboards (signs that could be placed on highways, roads and freeways). The idea was to supply these designs to whoever wanted to build billboards for Jesus. Actually, the brochure that we printed was called **Billboards for Jesus**, and we had several different designs—or styles and sizes—of billboards from which people could choose to build.

People could decide whether they wanted to build a mini billboard like 5 feet by 5 feet, or a maxi billboard like 8 feet by 24 feet—there were seven style sizes—and we would provide them with designs—certified by a registered public engineer—which gave them easy **how-to-do-it** instructions plus a detailed material list.

One retired US Air Force Colonel in the North East part of the United States financed the placement of five billboards himself. Miracles attended to these billboards because the Word of God—or a Bible message—was on each billboard. We let the people choose their own message, but we gave them some suggestions as to what to put on them.

During the time we were doing the **Billboards for Jesus** I was teaching at a Graduate School of Theology. I would allow people to come into our class and audit the classes or just to visit.

The father of one of my students in the seminary owned a liquor store. As I remember I think he owned two or three liquor stores. The student's father was not a Christian but he loved to come and hear the Word of God and also see the miracles that happened in the class I was teaching. We had many real miracles that happened in our classes as a result of the Holy Spirit's presence and because of the Word of God being taught.

This particular individual that owned the liquor stores happened to own some land in an area called Lake Isabella in California. He donated this land—or gave us permission to use this land—to put up a billboard for the Lord Jesus. We gathered some volunteers together and following the plans that we had designed, we built a large billboard. We built it in sections, we had 6 different sections and the billboard was 24 feet long and it had a Gospel message.

We finished the sign plus the framing in a location about 180 miles from where the sign was to be placed next to a highway. However, we didn't assemble the 6 sections until we drove the trucks up to the area where we would install it. When we got there we realized we didn't really have access to that land and we would need to go through some neighbor's land or an adjoining property. We thought it best to go to the property owner to the left. It was a beauty shop, a beauty salon. The lady there who also lived on that property told us an amazing thing. She said, *"I had a vision of a billboard going up on that property. Yes, certainly, you can use my land and you can hook up to my electrical power."* That was another thing that we needed, electrical power. So there were THREE MIRACLES counting the liquor store owner who gave us the land to use.

We spent a great part of 1 day and into the second day working on the sign, assembling the six (6) panels to the frame. We drilled five giant holes in the earth to support the beams for the billboard. We installed the 6 sections together and then we put large concrete bricks in the bottom of the holes to support the weight of the beams. Now the bricks were square and, of course, the holes were round.

After we finished assembling the six sections of the billboard with the support beams on it **we realized a problem**. If we dropped the billboard into the holes and the support beams did not hit the square blocks—if any of the posts landed between the blocks and the periphery of the round holes—the sign would have been crooked and we had no way to pull that back up.

HERE IS A POWER PRINCIPLE

Plan as you can. Coordinate the logistics as you can. **When you get to where you can't go any farther, God will take you through**. Some people waste so much time trying to refine everything from the start that they never get anything done. If you know God has told you to do something, move forward doing what God has shown you to do. **When you need it, it will be there**. Exercise faith ... move forward in faith.

Our next big problem was that we didn't have anyway to lift the billboard. It was so heavy—actually, I had over-engineered it and it was so strong—we couldn't lift it and we couldn't incline it anywhere near vertical where the support poles would slide into the holes.

While we were praying and thinking, *"What are we going to do now? How can we lift the sign?"* I saw an Arco (gasoline) tanker truck driving across the property going around to the right side of the property, towards the rear of the land. The tanker truck—the fuel tanker truck—had a slanted surface on the back. In other words, the back of the tanker was not vertical, it was slanted approximately 60 degrees. **The light bulb went on in my mind**. I thought, *"What if we could lift—tilt—the sign high enough so the top of the billboard would be on the back side of the tanker and the tanker could back up and then slide the billboard up?"* Then we could drop it into the holes.

In other words, we would be using the back of the Arco tanker truck as an inclined plane. Well it was going to take **ANOTHER MIRACLE** for the driver of this truck to agree to do such a thing—especially with the legal implications. However, the driver said, *"Yes, I would be glad to do that."* We explained to him it was for the Lord Jesus, the Messiah of Israel, and it was going to proclaim the Word of God. The driver was happy and wanted to be blessed.

The driver backed the tanker truck into position, and we had enough manpower plus jacks to get the top of the billboard lifted up to where it would slide on the back of the tanker truck. I don't know what the driver was going to think if we scratched the back of the truck as the sign was sliding up but somehow we cushioned it so it didn't rub off with friction.

As the driver backed the truck up, the sign began to lift up vertically. All of a sudden the sign with the support beams fell exactly into the holes where they should be—AND did NOT go to either side of the concrete blocks, but fell perfectly on to each of the concrete blocks in the center of each hole.

THIS SIGN REACHED MANY THOUSANDS OF PEOPLE FOR MANY YEARS

Then guess what happened. A large denomination—a Christian denomination—bought the property a few years later and the first thing they did was tear down the sign that was there for the Lord Jesus. My friend, don't get religious—**please**—just love the Lord. *"Delight* *yourself in the Lord he will give you the desires of your heart."* (Psalm 37:4)

Isn't it amazing that a man that owned liquor stores let us use the land so that the Lord Jesus could be glorified and His Word be proclaimed ... but years later a church comes along and takes the sign down. Now we know why Jesus' big conflict was not with the sinners—*not with the worldly people*—but **Jesus' conflict was with the religious crowd of His day.**

I hope this message about ***Miracles in Construction*** has helped you. Whatever sector of life you are involved in, try to include the Word of God—put out the Word of God. You have this promise that can NOT fail: *"So is my word that goes out from My mouth; it does not return to me empty. Instead, it does what I want, and accomplishes what I purpose."* (Isaiah 55:11)

Forget about religion. Love people and let the power—the love and the healing of the Lord Jesus—flow through you to touch lives where you are ... and then let it be multiplied by prayer—in faith—around the world.

MIRACLES AT THE JERUSALEM HILTON

In this chapter I want to talk to you today about **listening to God**. Reading the news today about Israel and Jerusalem—and the forces against them trying to destroy them—my mind kept rolling over the great victories that God has given Israel in the past. My friend, if you want to experience great victories in your personal life, then help Israel

The Bible tells us, *"Pray for the peace of Jerusalem. They will prosper that love her."* (Psalm 122:6) If you want to be blessed, help the Jews—get on God's side. **Don't be against God or you'll be on the losing side, and don't be against Israel or you'll be on the losing side**.

I was driving down the street in Jerusalem and going by—at that time—the new Jerusalem Hilton Hotel (now the Waldorf Astoria). It was snowing. It was kind of a light snow in March as I remember. Driving by the hotel, the Spirit of God spoke to me and said, *"I want you to go in the hotel and book facilities, and I want you to hold a seminar for Messiah."*

What I want to speak to you specifically about NOW is **listening to the voice of God ... listening to the Spirit of God.** And I will relate to that by telling you about *Miracles at the Jerusalem Hilton.*

I went in to the hotel and I was directed to the Sales Manager, a man named Ya'akov Avneri (Jacob Avneri). As we met and discussed the seminar I wanted to hold, he asked me, *"What is it that you want to do at the seminar?"* I told him that I was a believer in the Mashiach—in the Messiah Yeshua—and I wanted to hold meetings for both Jews and Arabs: for whoever wanted to come. He was a little—well, maybe a lot—hesitant. We began to talk and finally I noticed a college ring on Jacob's hand, and I said, *"Ya'akov, where did you go to university?"* He said, *"At the University of Nevada in Las Vegas,"* and I said, *"I used to live in Las Vegas."*

We began to talk back and forth and we started really enjoying one another, and finally Ya'akov told me, *"You know what? I'm going to lease you the facilities,"* he said, *"but there's one condition,"* and I said, *"What's that?"* He said, *"You're going to have to allow us to do the catering."* But even before that, the Holy Spirit had instructed me, *"Whatever he says to you, do it. Agree with it,"* so I said, *"Well, how much will that cost me, Jacob?"*

He began to tell me the price for catering and I'm like, *"Whoa. The facilities are expensive enough,"* and I remembered what God told me by His Spirit. The Holy Spirit had told me, *"Whatever he says, do it. No matter what the cost."* I said, *"Okay, Jacob, go ahead and cater the facilities."*

So I had a seminar at the Jerusalem Hilton, and without any press release or advertising, other than word of mouth. God brought in Jews and Arabs, and all kinds of people. It was a tremendous seminar and the Spirit of God began ministering in His gifts when I begin to share about Yeshua (Jesus). **The LORD was present with miraculous healings**.

I remember one United Nations officer who came to the meetings. He was a Major in the UN. The Lord gave me a Word of Knowledge for him. If you don't know what the Word of Knowledge is, it's where the Holy Spirit shows you a situation about someone or something. He reveals that situation—not to embarrass the person—but to let them know that God knows about them and loves them and wants to help them. I gave the Word of Knowledge the LORD had given me for this man—the United Nations officer—and he was dumbfounded. He was miraculously healed, and then the Lord baptized him in the Holy Spirit and he spoke in a new language—in tongues—the language of the Spirit. He spoke in tongues like we read about in the Jewish New Testament—the B'rit Chadashah—in the *Book of Acts*, Chapter Two.

Later, that United Nations officer was able to get materials out of the country—out of Israel—to me and into the United States. From those materials, I was able to reach tens of thousands of wonderful Jewish people in the land of Israel. A while later, a Jewish man called me from San Francisco. He was from Tiberias, Israel. He had a business in Tiberias. I was in my publishing house when he phoned. I don't know how he knew to contact me because I had an unlisted phone number.

The man told me, *"I will pay anything to meet you,"* so I told him, *"I'll meet you Thursday morning in the lobby of the Disneyland Hotel in Anaheim, California."* When he came in, I recognized him from his description—what he would be wearing and so forth—so we went out to the rear of the main lobby where all the water pools are. I talked to him for two hours from the Tanakh (the Hebrew Scriptures, the Old Testament). I shared with him the scriptures dealing with the Mashiach, and the Lord opened his eyes—opened his heart—and he saw the light and received Yeshua (Jesus) as his Messiah.

He was so happy, and he pulled out of his briefcase a piece of literature that we had sent to his daughter in Israel. He was probably in his early '60s. His daughter was raised and had her own family. As a result of the United Nations officer being healed and baptized in God's wonderful Spirit—speaking in tongues—and getting materials out of Israel for us to reach people in Israel, this man's daughter had received one of the pieces of literature we distributed in Israel.

After about six weeks, she took it to her father. They both **realized it was a sign from God** and that's why her father came all the way to the United States. Again, I never found out how he got my phone number, I forgot to ask him. He received Jesus as his Messiah and then I took him back to the concierge where he changed his flight. He flew immediately back to Jerusalem.

It's important to listen to the Holy Spirit. Listen to God when He speaks to you. **God may also give you an idea**. It may not be an idea for you—it may be an idea for you to share with someone. We should be good stewards of the ideas that God gives us, so listen to the Voice of God, and then do what God tells you.

Obey Him, and then God will use you to help others. **God will do miracles for you and multiply them through you for others around the world**.

HOW TO TRAVEL WITH MIRACLES

In this chapter I want to share with you about walking with God—literally—actually, about hitchhiking with God. I had just finished a period of graduate studies in school back east. I was praying and asking God where to go. I had nowhere to go and I actually had no money. I don't think I even had a dollar—if I had that.

After I had prayed that morning I asked God, *"Show me where to go."* I went to the post office box at the school. I picked up my mail and when I opened up a letter, there was part of a map. It had been cut out in a circle with pinking sheers, the scissors a garment maker uses to cut fabric.

That map contained a county area in Alabama in the United States. The map was about ten inches wide. In that map was a line—a black line—that had been drawn with an "X" and a red circle around the "X." I knew exactly where that was. I said, *"God, I asked you to show me where you wanted me to go. This map is such a sign. I can't deny it. The only problem is ... I don't have any money."*

Within about an hour—*nobody knowing that I didn't have any money*—I received money from two different sources in cash. If I remember correctly, that money came from fellow students at the school. It was enough money to ride the bus half way to the location shown by the "X" on the map.. I forget how I got the other half of the way. I had been there one time before and held a revival. During that revival, a man in that area had shot his wife, kicked her out of the truck, and left her in a ditch beside the road.

I was told about the shooting immediately after an evening service, I went to the hospital. There was no way I could get into the hospital. Crowds of people were out in front and nobody was allowed in. I assume maybe a doctor could have gotten in—but **I remembered how Jesus just walked through a crowd one time. I just started to walk and I walked right into the hospital**. I walked right into the intensive care ward where the lady was who had been shot. I didn't even know what the lady's name was. As I remember she had been shot by her husband four times. **I prayed for her and left**.

During these meetings, every afternoon we hooked up a large loudspeaker. The horn on that loudspeaker must have been 18 inches wide—about a half a meter wide—in diameter. For about three hours in the afternoon I would preach something and then we'd play a song. We blasted it. We were about a half a block from the city courthouse and the jail. The power of God invaded that community. It was a town named Double Springs, Alabama.

That next day, after I had prayed with the lady in the hospital I went to visit her husband in jail. **God had spared her life.** In the jail, I got to see the man who had shot his wife, kicked her out of the truck and left her to die in the ditch. I talked to him about Jesus. I never heard somebody yell so loudly in my life. **He cried out, begging God to forgive him, and he repented. He gave his life to the Messiah, Jesus.**

So, here I was, returning to that same area after graduate school. Why? **Because God had sent me a map with an "X" and a red circle around the "X."** I later realized I had NOT finished the work I should have the time I was there before. One little boy had been saved and on this return trip I baptized him in the Sipsey River. That little boy was the son of the lady who had been shot. I went to their home. The lady, the husband, and the little boy were all serving God. Praise God's holy name. Baruch Hashem.

When I left that area I had no money and I was hitchhiking on my way up to Pennsylvania from Double Springs, Alabama. It was getting rather cool in the evening and I only had a jacket—with a shirt on underneath that jacket. The last ride in that late afternoon let me out on a little two-lane highway. I said, *"God, I don't even know where I'm at and there's nobody even here to pick me up to take me where I need to go."*

I was about 900 miles (1450 kilometers) from where I needed to be and **I start complaining to God**. I was cold and it was getting late in the afternoon. **Then all of a sudden I started to praise God**. I thought, *"God knows how to take care of me. He's done it in the past, he can do it again."* When I started praising God, I just felt impressed to turn around. I was beside a hill that went down from the highway. I looked down that hill and even though it was bright green grass—like most grass is in Alabama—I saw another clump of green stuff.

I went down there—and surely enough—there was a handful of money. I said, *"Praise God. Heavenly Father, you let me out in the perfect spot."* I was able to use that money for a motel and travel on the next day. God is so good. That's what I'm talking to you about: walking with God … hitchhiking with God. I don't care if you're flying with God. **Whatever you're doing, God will show you—lead you and guide you—if you listen to him AND obey him.**

My friend, it doesn't matter where you're at or what situation you're in, **God will take care of you IF you trust Him**. He loves you. God isn't some big ogre in Heaven waiting to hit you with a big stick—and neither is he some old gray haired man sitting in a rocking chair. **God is eternally young and he's with it**. You can never con God. In the Holy Bible God tells us, *"I will lead you and guide you with my eye upon you. Just like a horse with a bridle in his mouth, I will guide you."* (Psalm 32)

God tells us that he will even guide us to our old age when our hair is gray and white.

> *"Even to your old age and gray hairs I am He who will sustain you. I have made you and I will carry you; I will carry you and I will rescue you."*
>
> – Isaiah 46:4

Your father in heaven even knows when a sparrow falls to the ground dead. He knows every detail about your life. He made you. He made this whole universe. Trust Him today. Pray. **Ask God to show you what he wants you to do—and then obey him.**

If you don't have the facilities, or the means, or the logistics to carry out what God wants you to do, then ask God to give you what you need to carry out His plan. Then move ahead. Take the first step. Go. **When you go in faith, the miracles will happen**.

I trust this teaching will help you to know how to walk, fly, transport in space—whatever you do—with God. He loves you. My friend, **let God talk through you**. Tell your friends—even your enemies—about the wonderful Jesus, the Messiah of Israel: The Anointed One.

CRASH LANDING MIRACLES

One time I was flying to Los Angeles International Airport. It was a beautiful day. Let me back up a little. I had been away for three weeks. I had been down in Mexico in the Mainland—way down in the jungles—training pastors and holding seminars under thatched roofs with a tremendous bunch of brothers and sisters in the LORD. I worked through interpreters.

Then after that I flew to Chicago where I held several meetings. There were several MIRACLES and the LORD really blessed me. I was flying back to L.A. and it was early morning—about 10:00 AM Pacific Time—and I had a pocketful of money. As we were approaching the airport for landing, we were circling over the ocean. While I looked down at the water, the plane was kind of tilted and I thought, *"What a beautiful day"*—I was kind of joking to the Lord—and I said, *"God, if there's any day I don't want to go into the water, it's today. I'd like to get to the bank first."*

Well, God must have a tremendous sense of humor because I noticed the plane kept going around and around and around the airport. Finally, the captain of the aircraft came on the loud speaker and notified us that one of the landing gears was not down. He said, *"We're going to have to fly in near the tower so they can do a visual examination and let us know whether the landing gear is down or not."*

We flew in near the tower and—sure enough—the captain comes back on and he says, ***"The landing gear***

is not down. We are going to have to prepare for a crash landing." The flight attendants had us take our shoes off and gave us all pillows. They collected our shoes and stowed them. Then, they instructed us to lay the pillow flat on our lap, but lay our head sideways and stay in that position to prepare for a crash landing.

While I'm doing that, the Lord spoke to me and He said, **"Son, if you will pray out loud in tongues, I will bring the landing gear down."** Well, my first thought was, *"People will think I'm crazy if I pray out loud in tongues on this airplane."* My second thought was this, *"It would be better than dying."*

So I obeyed God—I started praying in tongues out loud. The lady across the aisle next to me asked me what I was doing. I explained to her what God told me. I prayed with her and she gave her to life to Jesus, the Messiah. Check this out: before we hit the ground—as a result of praying in the Holy Spirit's language—the landing gear came down—*just as God promised me*—and we affected a safe landing.

There's a truth here. **The spiritual controls the physical—the material—world**. That's why Yeshua taught us, *"Truly, I say to you, whosoever shall say to this mountain, 'You be removed and be cast into the sea,' and shall not doubt in his heart but shall believe that those things which he says shall come to pass, he shall have whatever he says."* (Mark 11;23)

Notice in that verse **three times Jesus mentioned "saying"** and only one time mentioned "believing." You can believe whoever you want or whatever you want, but I believe what Jesus said. **The spiritual rules the material—or, the physical—world**.

When I obeyed God and prayed in the language of the Holy Spirit, He brought the landing gear down in that big jet airplane. When you pray in tongues, in the language of the Spirit, you're praying according to the will of God. You're praying secret truths to God, the Father. The Bible tells us in 1 Corinthians 14:2 that you're praying **secret truths** to the Father. *"For he who speaks in a tongue does not speak to men but to God, for no one understands him; however, in the spirit he speaks secret truths."*

My friend, you never know what's going to happen to you at any given day. Things may be going just super nice and it's a beautiful day—just like it was on that airplane. Everything seems to be going just right—all of a sudden something may happen unexpectedly from left field. That's why it's important to be prayed up all the time. **Move in faith, speak the Word of God and pray in the language of the Holy Spirit—in tongues—and use the name of Jesus**.

Now, my friend, you know how to prepare for a crash landing.

CHILDREN AND MIRACLES – EEKS!

I want to talk to you in this part of the book about kids—about children—about young people. You know, if God would have judged most of us about what we did when we were young kids, we would be in the trash can. You know, I was thinking about some things I did when I was a kid that would have caused me to go absolutely ballistic if some kid—or one of my children—had done the same to me.

I remember, when I was a kid, there used to be trucks in which the drivers appeared to stand up while driving, and the trucks had open doors. They delivered milk and other things. I was always amazed by them, so I invented an "imagination" truck like them.

My parents had just installed new carpeting in the living room and dining room. I was in the dining room one morning driving my imaginary truck ... the kind with the open door like I described to you, where the driver would seem to stand up while he was driving. I was probably around the age of four. **I hopped out of the truck and I urinated on the new carpet**. Then I hopped back in the truck and shifted gears in my imaginary truck and took off again.

It wasn't long until my father—bless his heart—came into the room. He had been outdoors. He said, *"Who did that? What happened here?"* I said, *"Daddy, the dog did it."* I had had two dogs. One died and I had another. Both of them were named "Spot." Not very creative, I'll grant you. I said, *"Daddy, the dog did that. Spot did that."* My father commenced to grab the dog and rub his nose in the urine on the carpet and beat him with a newspaper and ... afterward cleaned up the mess while I kept messing around in my imaginary truck. You know, I was thinking about that. That would have driven me absolutely off the chart if that had happened to me. **I don't know how God can put up with the stupid things we've done—and still do—in our lives**.

I remember another time my parents were redecorating the kitchen. They had installed brand new linoleum flooring. They were painting and doing the trim, too. There was a full gallon of bright green paint on the kitchen counter. I thought I'd help them—it looked like the lid was fastened. I picked up the gallon of paint and put it on my shoulder. Wouldn't you know—the top wasn't fastened on it—it went all down my back, and the whole gallon went onto the brand new linoleum flooring. My father and mother must have had very cushioned hearts, because I don't see how they kept from having heart attacks right then.

I was thinking today about reaching children—reaching kids—reaching young people. I remember one time I had been ministering in the open air in downtown Los Angeles. I don't know why, but I decided to go home a completely different way ... maybe because of traffic or whatever. **I ended up in a city where I had never been**. There's over 12 million people in the greater L.A. metropolitan area. I ended up that day in a city suburb where I'd never been. I got lost in a residential neighborhood—wanting to get home—and hungry.

While I was driving down the street—all of a sudden—some kids jerked up a rope in front of my car. There was a kid on one side and a kid on the other side and a bunch of kids hanging around. **I slammed on my brakes and the kids ran**. They were laughing and having fun, but **I was so mad**. I was really burning up. I decided, *"I'm going to drive around the block and tell those kids what I'm thinking."* I drove around the block, made several turns, came back and I found them. **Then the Lord told me, *"Don't you dare get mad at those kids. Remember what you used to be like, and what you used to do."***

The Lord prompted me, ***"Don't get mad at these kids. I want you to talk to them about Jesus."*** I invited one boy who had pulled the rope up to come to the car. I wasn't even parked. He came up to my car and I said, *"I want to give you something."* I said, *"Has anybody ever told you about Jesus?"*

You know what the young boy said to me? Think about this: I'm in a metroplex area where I had never been in one of the cities around L.A., and **this kid says to me, *"Are you Brother Handley?"*** I about fell out of my car. I said, **"Yes, how do you know?"** He said, ***"Oh, I didn't really know, but last night I was in another city and a man told me about you—and how you loved God—and what you did, and how God does MIRACLES through you."***

I said, *"Well did he tell you about Jesus?"* He said, *"Yes."* **He said, *"I received Jesus last night."*** I said, *"Well did he tell you about the Baptism in the Holy*

Spirit?" He said, *"No, he didn't."* I explained to him clearly how to receive the Baptism in the Spirit. **I laid my hands on his head—I was still in my car and he was standing outside—and the Spirit of God came upon him, and another language came out of his mouth**. He was having the Bible experience of speaking in tongues that we read about in the Jewish New Testament in the *Book of Acts*, Chapter Two.

Here I was, lost in a completely different area—never been in that city before—and God crossed my path with one young man who had received Messiah Jesus the night before, but had not received the Baptism in the Holy Spirit of God. God knows what's going on in our lives. **He knows the little details**. He has the hairs of our head numbered. He's has our tears in a bottle. He knows when one sparrow falls to the ground dead. My friend, **there's nothing that God doesn't know about your life—and He loves you**. He cares for you, just as much as He does for a little child.

Reach out to the children, my friend. Reach out to the young people. If you reach young people, you're **reaching the next generation**. If you reach young people, **you're reaching the mass of the population**. In most countries, 50 percent of the population is under the age of 15 ... so you're reaching the mass of the populace. Also, when you reach young people, **you're reaching somebody that has a whole lifetime to serve the LORD**.

My friend, God is a loving God. He's a forgiving God. I'm glad He has forgiven me—not only of my sins—but all the stupid junk I did when I jumped out of my imaginary truck and urinated on my father's new carpet ... and when I spilled a whole gallon of paint on the new flooring my parents had just installed in the kitchen. **After all the stupid things that we've done—and are still doing—God still loves us**. He's a loving God. He's a good Father. I had a wonderful father and a wonderful mother, but our Father in Heaven outshines any parents here on earth.

My friend, **whatever you're going through today, God knows the details**. You may not be a young person, but you can be young in your heart. As a matter of fact, the Holy Bible tells us that unless we become like little children, we cannot enter the Kingdom of Heaven. If you haven't already, you can have that New Birth today. And if you have—maybe like that young boy on the street, when they pulled up the rope in front of my car—you need the Baptism in the Holy Spirit. Just pray and ask Messiah Jesus to come into your heart and to pour out His Spirit upon you. **He will give you power, and then YOU can reach the young people of the world**.

**We recommend the following
companion books to this book:**

Action Keys for Success

Success Cycles and Secrets

How to Do Great Works

Faith and Quantum Physics

Available at Amazon and other book stores

OTHER BOOKS BY PRINCE HANDLEY

- Map of the End Times
- How to Do Great Works
- Flow Chart of Revelation
- Action Keys for Success
- Health and Healing Complete Guide to Wholeness
- Prophetic Calendar for Israel & the Nations: Thru 2023
- Healing Deliverance
- How to Receive God's Power with Gifts of the Spirit
- Healing for Mental and Physical Abuse
- Victory Over Opposition and Resistance
- Healing of Emotional Wounds
- How to Be Healed and Live in Divine Health
- Healing from Fear, Shame and Anger
- How to Receive Healing and Bring Healing to Others
- New Global Strategy: Enabling Missions
- The Art of Christian Warfare
- Success Cycles and Secrets
- New Testament Bible Studies (A Study Manual)
- Babylon the Bitch – Enemy of Israel
- Resurrection Multiplication – Miracle Production
- Faith and Quantum Physics – Your Future
- Conflict Healing – Relational Health
- Decision Making 101 – Know for Sure
- Total Person Toolbox
- Prophecy, Transition & Miracles
- Enhanced Humans – Mystery Matrix
- Israel and Middle East – Past Present Future
- Anarchy and Revolution – A Prophecy
- Real Miracles – For Normal People

AVAILABLE AT AMAZON AND OTHER BOOK STORES

In addition, check out the 99 cent FAST READ
Spiritual Growth Mini-Books by Prince Handley

SPIRITUAL GROWTH SERIES

UNIVERSITY OF EXCELLENCE PRESS
Los Angeles ▪ London ▪ Tel Aviv

BONUS

To help you, and to help you teach others, we have prepared FREE **Rabbinical Studies** at this site:

uofe.org/RABBINICAL_STUDIES.html

The above are commentaries from **ancient** Jewish Rabbis that identify the Mashiach of Israel.

Also, to help you, and to help you teach others, you will find Bible Studies in English, Spanish and French.

▪ English FREE Bible Studies

uofe.org/english_bible_studies.html

▪ Spanish FREE Bible Studies

uofe.org/spanish_bible_studies.html

▪ French FREE Bible Studies

uofe.org/french_bible_studies.html

LIVE A LIFE OF EXCELLENCE

Email for seminars to:
princehandley@gmail.com

UNIVERSITY OF EXCELLENCE PRESS
Los Angeles ▪ London ▪ Tel Aviv

+

NOTE

We listen to our readers. Tell us what **new** subject matter you would like to see published. Email your ideas to: universityofexcellence@gmail.com

www.ingramcontent.com/pod-product-compliance
Lightning Source LLC
Chambersburg PA
CBHW060707030426
42337CB00017B/2794